Two Brothers

A TRADITIONAL TALE FROM AFRICA

Retold by Jane Langford

Illustrated by Anne Wilson

Rigby

Long ago, in a small village in Africa, in a house made of red clay, there lived two brothers named Bwalo and Kamba. They were idle boys who never did any work. All day long, they just sat in the hot sun.

The people of the village grew more and more frustrated with the two brothers. One day, their laziness became too much for the village people.

"You are lazy to the bone!" said Uncle Obi. "You can't live in the village any longer."

"But we like it here!" protested Bwalo and Kamba.

"No. You are too selfish. You take things from the village, but you never give anything back. Now go away!" Uncle Obi raised his hand and pointed out across the African plains.

The two brothers looked at Uncle Obi, and they knew there was no use arguing. Later that very day, they left the village with nothing but a bag of corn.

While they walked, the brothers tried to think of ways they could get back in favor with the village.

"Let us plant the corn," suggested Kamba. "It will grow and we can give the crop to the village."

"Good idea," said Bwalo.

So, with their hopes raised, the brothers walked across the dusty African plains until they saw a lake. The land around it was fresh and green.

"Let us plant the corn here," they said.

So that is what the brothers did. Soon they would have something to give the village.

Now, under a kapok tree by the lake, in a
nest made of reeds, there lived two geese. Every
day, the geese hunted for food. One day, they
saw the lush green shoots of the brothers' corn.
They landed in the middle of it and ate until
they were full.

The two brothers saw the geese and quickly ran over to the corn, but they were too late. There was nothing left—not even a single green shoot.

"Oh no!" they cried with disappointment. "Our plan has been ruined! Now what will we give to the village?"

Not long after that, one of the geese settled down on her nest and laid an egg.

"What a beautiful egg!" said Bwalo.

"Yes!" said Kamba. "Let us wait until there are lots of eggs. They will hatch into a fine flock of goslings, and that would be a perfect gift for the village!"

Bwalo and Kamba worked hard. They
brought food and water for the goose while
she sat in her nest. Every day the goose
laid another egg, until there were twelve in
the nest. The brothers waited patiently for the
eggs to hatch. Soon they would have something
to give to the village.

The eggs lay safe and snug in the nest under the kapok tree. But the tree was old. When the wind blew, its branches creaked.

CRACK! SNAP! The kapok tree's biggest branch fell to the ground. The eggs beneath it were smashed and broken.

"Oh no!" cried the brothers in despair. "Our plan has been ruined! Now what will we give to the village?"

Bwalo looked at the fallen branch and saw a single scarlet blossom. "Soon the tree will be covered in blossoms," he said. "It will turn into a fine crop of soft white cotton."

"That would be a wonderful gift for the village!" said Kamba.

Every day the brothers watched the tree, and slowly the blossoms grew.

The brothers waited for the blossoms to turn into cotton. Soon there would be something to give to the village.

One day, a huge gray elephant came down to drink at the lake. He saw the kapok tree with its old cracked bark, and he walked over to it. Then the elephant started to scratch his rough back on the tree's trunk and branches. First one blossom fell, then another, until the elephant was covered in a shower of red petals.

The brothers ran over to the kapok tree, but there were no blossoms left to turn into fine white cotton.

"Oh no!" they cried in despair. "Our plan has been ruined! Now what will we give to the village?"

The brothers could think of nothing else to give to the village. They knew that they would have to stay away forever. They hung their heads and slowly walked back along the dusty road toward the village, to say their final goodbyes.

"What are you doing here?" asked Uncle Obi.

"We have come to say goodbye," said Bwalo. "We tried to find things to give to the village, but all our plans failed."

"What did you try to find?" asked
Uncle Obi.

"A harvest of corn, a flock of geese, and
a crop of soft white cotton," said Kamba.

"That is no good," said Uncle Obi. "What
we need is water. Our well has dried up
and if we don't find water soon, we will all
surely die."

"Water!" cried Bwalo with delight. "We know
where there is water!"

Bwalo and Kamba led Uncle Obi to the lake. The water was fresh and clear.

Uncle Obi hugged the brothers. "Welcome home!" he said.

At last Kamba and Bwalo had found something to give back to the village!